SBN 978-1-4583-7286-4
90000
AF614124
9 781458 372864

About the Author

Reginald Levi Walker was born in rural Perry County in Alabama to the late Rev. R. Leon Walker, Jr. and Janie Mae Ward on July 9, 1964. He is the last of three children from this marriage. Reginald or Reggie, as he prefers to be called, was educated in the all black school system of rural Perry County. Reggie tried to excel at all his studies in School. He held memberships in the National Junior and Senior Honor Societies. In 1981, he moved to Miami, Florida to live with his mother. After graduating from American Senior High School, he enlisted in the U. S. Army. However, because of the call to preach and the tremendous preaching tradition in the Walker family, Reggie soon found himself preaching instead of fighting wars.

The first influence to preach came from his grandfather, Rev Walker, Sr. At the age of nine; Reggie accepted the call to preach at Greenleaf Baptist Church in Alabama. After discharging from service in 1985, he studied under his father and other ministers in the African Methodist Episcopal Church. He was licensed to preach at St, John A.M.E. Church in Tulsa, Oklahoma ordained an elder at Bethel A.M.E. Church in North Little Rock Arkansas and educated at Shorter Junior College in Arkansas. Reggie first pastorate was at Derrick Chapel A.M.E. Church in Van Buren, Arkansas. Since then, he has pastured many churches in Alabama, Arkansas, Florida, and Oklahoma; He now resides in Dallas, Texas He works to encourage children of God everywhere to stand up and be the mighty men and women of God. His favorite saying is I am blessed just to be alive.

Reggie knows the importance of each day since he has been living with an incurable disease since 1987. However, he firmly believes, if he lives God get the glory and if he dies, God gets the blame. He gave his illness to God along time ago and refuses to worry about it anymore.

(Additional information about the meaning of Nabahood23)

Not
Anger
But
Action will solve the problems of our neighbor
H
O
O
D
23 stands for the 23rd Psalms.

P.S. 23 stands for 'God loves you; therefore, I love you, too.'

The type of person needed for times like these

There is a great need for us to become the type of human being that our simple existence in these tedious times demands from us. Although, the belief in God is often mistakenly seen as a requirement for people to do good deeds, it is not a required ingredient needed to be a good person. In order for a person to be good, it takes simple actions. To be a good person, it only requires simple sincere communications from us that reveal that we care about other people in our world. To be a good person, it only requires us to see those we pass on the road of life as more than just objects to be used and abused. It requires us to see them as our brothers and sisters. More importantly, it requires us to see them as fellow human beings. However, being a good person is just an illusion of the type of person that is needed in these tedious times.

God created us to be more than just good people because even good people can go to hell. God created us to be more than just meaningless Christians, Jews, or Muslims. The true child of God is designed to be the representation of the powerful God that created us. We are designed to be more than just good. We are designed to be very good. We are called to be our brother and sister's keeper. We are called to be more than conquerors. We are taught to lay down our lives to help someone along the way. The real child of God is designed not only to give the lonely homeless person a ride down the road. We are designed to bring them into our own homes. We are designed to feed them from our tables and house them under our roofs. We are designed to touch the loveless lives around us with the abundant love that God has shown to us.

See the things that are good about a person that is a Christian, a Jew, a Muslim or other or no religion are just ordinary for a child of God. This is because a child of God is really a peculiar person. However, the difference between a good person and a child of God is not because we are labeled as Christian, Jewish, or Muslim. The difference is like the Good Samaritan, a child of God does not need a label to help those along the road. We will lay down our lives to put other's hurting lives back together. Remember, not all good people are Christians, Jews, or Muslims. In addition, all Christians, Jews, or Muslims are not all good people. Moreover, not all Christians, Jewish, or Islamic people are children of God. However, the children of God are all very good people because God is an extremely good God.

Therefore, in these hours of desperation and hopelessness, there stand a need for us to evolve into the type of people needed by God. In these tedious times where financial ruins and economic hardships have robbed us of the necessities of our daily lives, there stand a need for the very good people to come to the rescue of those hurt along the highway to the great American Dream. There stand a need for the children of God to come out of the church buildings and rescue the wounded travelers that are lying hurt along the road of life. There stand a need for us to become our brothers and sisters keepers. In these tedious and desperate times, there stand a need for us to become more than an illusion of what God created us to be. It is time for us to become the Good Samaritans that will stop and help those that has been hurt along the way.

Evicted but not abandoned

Early this morning, I sat looking into the dark sky and the verses from Psalm 30: 5 entered my mind. I watched the shadows of darkness flee from the coming morning light and heard the word of God speak, 'For his anger endures but a moment; in his favor is life.' Suddenly, the noise of daybreak replaced the silence of nighttime, and the word of God continued to say, 'weeping may endure for a night, but joy comes in the morning.'

God does get angry with us. Like a parent, God gets angry when His children are disobedient. We are disobedient to God when we do not follow the path toward righteousness given to us in His Holy Word. Like Adam and Eve, we know what the word of God has to say. However, we must read it for ourselves. We are disobedient when we allow Lucifer to trick us into doing the things God told us not to do. If we do not depend on man's interpretation and understanding of what God told us to do and just do it, God will guide our path. He will order the very steps of the righteous man, woman, and child of God down the pathway of life.

Therefore, God is rightfully angry with us. Although there are numerous reasons for His anger, the most pressing is our constant denial to be what He designed us to be. Of all of God's creation, man is the most like the creator. The most powerful entity in existence created humans in His image and likeness. When we deny the existence of God, our creator, we foolishly deny all the potentials and abilities that come with being a child of the most powerful entity in existence. Because of this, we have potentials and abilities that remain untapped.

Nevertheless, why would we not want to be like the one who created us? Our motivation not to be all that God created us to be is simple to explain. We refuse to be like

God because we think it takes too much effort. We think it takes too much effort to love a person, so we choose to hate them instead. However, to hate, we must find a reason. We must look for a cause of dislike to rally behind. We must muster all our envy, strife, and stress, and then we must hate. Nevertheless, to love, we only have to look to our creator and do what He did. Although Adam and Eve gave Him a reason to hate, God loved them instead.

Additionally, God loves us in spite of our sins because there is a limit to God's anger. Adam and Eve did sin, and God did evict them from paradise; still, God did not abandon them. He created a world just for them. God sacrificed one of His creations and covered Adam and Eve bare skin. Since they decided they were big enough to do what they wanted, God sent them on their way. God put them out of the garden of Humanities Beginnings to do what He designed them to do. Since Adam and Eve broke the house rules, God put them out of the garden to take over the world. However, God did not continue to be angry with them. He put them out of the garden; but He never left them alone.

This is because God is the God of Favor. God shows us kindness everyday because He wakes us from our sleep. God loves us and gives us a generous portion of His grace and mercy to be able to feed, clothe ourselves, and exist in our right mind. However, God's favor or goodwill goes farther than we expect it should. For God so loved the world that He gave His only begotten son. That personal sacrifice or unexpected display of favor from God is more than we could ever expect. It is certainly more than we are ready to display to others ourselves.

Of course, every human is favored to some degree by God. Besides the obvious benefits of joy and righteousness, the presence of God's favor lengthens the days of our life. God's favor allows us to achieve more than we could accomplish in the regular span of our lifetime. God's favor gives us long life because God protects and shelters us under His care. Though thousands gets sick and die and in spite of the tens of thousands choosing to kill themselves, God favors us with long life, unmovable peace, and a good understanding that God's goodness and mercy will be with us all of our lives. The more we please God, the more he will favor us. However, God's favor is not material or worldly. God's favor is a spiritual blessing that we obtain by praying to God, seeking His face, and keeping the commandments of the Lord.

Adam, Adam where fore art thou Adam?

Began, birth, commence, start; these words are refreshing as well as optimistic. Whether used to refer to the beginning of a new day, the birth of a child, the commencement of a long awaited vacation, or the start of a symphony, these encouraging words are full of promise and free of problems. They immediately stir hopes and awaken visions of the future. The word, Genesis, means beginning or origin and it unfolds the record of the beginning of the world, human history, family, civilization, and salvation.

The book of Genesis begins with God. It begins with God creating the world in a majestic and awe-inspiring display of power and purpose. This divine demonstration brought about the birth of man and then woman in the Garden of Eden. They were specifically crafted in the image and likeness of God. In the book of Genesis, we are told the story of God's divine purpose and righteous plan for His creation, His creatures, and man. In the book of Genesis, the person and nature of God is revealed. In the book of Genesis, the position and characteristics of men are shown. Accordingly, the consequences of sin are revealed forcing the promise and the assurance of salvation to commence as the world and man is hurled into an unexpected meeting with Lucifer. Because of this resulting encounter, God's once flawless creation soon starts to shatter and man's close knit fellowship with God is torn apart.

Although Genesis is full of intriguing stories, let us examine the fascinating characters and world changing events of the most dramatic love story ever written. For the first time ever, casted in the position of leading man and woman were none other than Adam and Eve. God assigned them to tend the garden, care for one another, and to have dominion over everything He created. Casted in the role, as villain of this story is none other than Lucifer. This same Lucifer played the leading character in trying to overthrow God.

Just for a brief moment let me stop because there is something needing to be mentioned before we continue with this story. As the children of God, we need not fear Lucifer because the Scriptures inform us that he has already been defeated. Nevertheless as the children of God, we must respect who Lucifer was, is, and what he stands for now. Lucifer is a spirit or an angel made by God. Because he turned against God, there is nothing good about him. Lucifer is a jealous, crafty, and a very dangerous spirit but he is also a very intelligent spirit.

The Scriptures plainly inform us that Lucifer can be a roaring lion or an angel of light; however, for this role he came as a simple snake in the grass. Lucifer realized that if he came as himself, he would be easily recognized and his well thought out plans would be spoiled. Lucifer knew that man named the newly created snake in Genesis 2: 19-22. He knew the snake would not scare them away, because they knew or was familiar with it. Lucifer's main tactic has always been to use something familiar to man to get to man. Today, Lucifer is still easily getting to us in the same way.

Lucifer uses appealing things, interesting ideals, engaging thoughts, and influential people we are familiar with, use to, and know to get to us. Through the religious leaders, he convinced Judas to sell Jesus for thirty pieces of silver. Lucifer used the wicked ideal of racial superiority to kill millions of innocent people. He used the acceptable concept of the right to bear arms and the practice of more firepower, more peace to destroy our peace and make this world a dangerous place to live.

Nevertheless, because Eve was familiar with the snake, she allowed herself to take the introductory step into sin. The never-ending journey toward sin is an unchanging process that began with the simple innocent act of listening. Simply listening in itself is not a sin, but Eve conceived the sin when knowingly listened to words not of God. Up to the point of her misguided conversation with the snake, the only voice she heard in the garden other than Adam's was the voice of God. She knew that the voice coming across the lips of the snake was not the voice of Adam and it was not the voice of God. She knew the voice coming out of the mouth of that snake was not the snake's voice, because when God created snakes, he did not design them to talk. Still, in the midst of the amazingly breathtaking garden on that dreadful day, Eve stood and intentionally listened to the strangely evil voice of Lucifer anyway.

Even now, we continue to fall for the same tricks of Lucifer. We are acquainted with what the Scriptures say; nevertheless, in spite of everything we claim to know, we continue to listen to the untrue words of Lucifer and his many deceiving prophets. We know the Scriptures instruct us to seek first the kingdom of God and His righteousness, nevertheless we continue to seek first our own prosperity and riches. We know the Scriptures say that by Jesus' stripes we are healed, nevertheless we continue to seek first the doctor and his bags of pills. We know the Scriptures tell us to discipline our children, however we continue to listen to Dr. this and Dr. that and our children are running wild. We know the Scriptures instruct us to bring our tithes into God's storehouse, however, we rather take our money to Bally's, or the Indian Nations casinos and return home broke, disgusted, and deceived. Every day, Lucifer is busy deceiving us because we are constantly acting like Eve. We are acquainted with and know what the word of God says, but intentionally we rather listen to the mind numbing words of Lucifer instead.

The next fatal step on the journey toward sin is in the agreement with Lucifer. Sadly, in Genesis 3:2-3 we discover that Eve knew the exact words God commanded and easily repeated them to the snake. She had no excuse for not doing the right thing because she knew exactly what God wanted her to do. Nevertheless, instead of seeking God, resisting Lucifer and watching him flee, she agreed with the false information given to her by the snake. Today, we are still agreeing with Lucifer's false information. When the misguided voice of society tells us that pre-martial sex is okay, we agree regardless that God called it a sin. Every time the self serving voices of the media suggest that there is nothing wrong with a little bump and grind, that it is okay to be married and still fool around, we agree, nevertheless, God still called it adultery and it is a sin. Even as the lying voices of our politicians, movie stars, and music stars proclaim that it is okay to be gay, we agree, however in spite of everything we say, legislate, or do, God still called it an abomination and it is a sin. When our religious leaders, family, friends, and running friends state that it is okay to hate, kill, steal, and destroy based on a lie, we agree. However, hopefully, some day we will realize that God still says, "Thou shall not." and that means it is a sin.

The final step into the valley of sin was in the unwise premeditated action of Eve and then Adam. According to Genesis 3:6, Eve listened, agreed, and then acted upon the evil advice of Lucifer. Mesmerized by his clever and exciting words, she turned and deliberately strolled up to the forbidden tree. She looked at how desirable and delicious the outlawed fruit on the large flourishing tree appeared and made the biggest mistake of her young life. Willingly choosing to disobey God, Eve's trembling hand reached out, grabbed one of the ripe fruit that was hanging just within her reach and took a bite. After that initial sinful action, she brought someone in on her sin. Eve immediately turned and gave some of the ill-gotten food to her husband who was with her and he did eat. The very moment they recklessly acted upon the evil suggestion of Lucifer all the powers of the Prince of Hell was let loose on God's once perfect creation. After Adam and Eve sinned, they were instantly evicted from their garden home. After they sinned, they promptly lost their fellowship with God. After they committed only their first sin, nothing on the biosphere called earth would be the same.

In the cool of the evening, our all-knowing and merciful God came out for his usual walk in the garden. However, on this particular day as He looked around, He noticed that things did not seem the same. The colorful arrangement of flowers was not as brilliant and his beloved man did not come out to meet him. Maybe, the man and the woman was busy doing something somewhere inside the enormous garden. God's Spirit turned the corner by the huge mountain and inquisitively peered out across the grassy plains. However, man, his most prized creation was nowhere to be found. Listen as the caring voice of God vibrates among the growing green trees and echoes across the snow covered mountain range. God called out to His beloved, "Adam, Adam, where fore art thou, Adam." That one day has been recorded as the saddest day in human history. That day was sad not just because, Adam and Eve were evicted from a one of a kind paradise. That day was sad because on that day man broke the heart of God. Adam responded, "I'm hiding, I'm hiding because I was afraid you would see my nakedness. I'm hiding because I was afraid you would see my sin."

As the scene quickly changes from the past to the present century in which we live, we discover that we now inhabit a world scarred by centuries of neglect, abuse, and pain. Just a decade ago, we bid goodbye an unforgettable century that witnessed four wars and dozens of smaller conflicts. We left behind a horrifying century where we killed each other because of hatred, racial differences, or the color of a shirt worn. Now we stand at the beginning of a new century that has already buried millions of its citizens because of genocide, famine, disease, and unpredictable storms. Over this first decade, we have witness America descend from being the home of the free and land of the brave to barring ourselves inside our homes because it has become too dangerous in the streets.

Nevertheless, God is still calling out to us in this mad psychopathic jungle. God's voice continues to vibrate off our forest of towering buildings and flow down our rivers of streets. God is calling out in our cities, towns, and communities. He is calling out to each of us. He is calling mothers, fathers, sisters, and brothers. God is calling, " Adam, Adam, where fore art thou, Adam." He is not calling out for our physical location. He is seeking our spiritual location. He is not calling out for our physical condition. He is calling out for our spiritual condition. Can you hear His concerned voice calling, "Adam, Adam, where fore art thou, Adam."

God is calling out to the church, which is the body of Christ. However, we are hiding. We are hiding behind our traditions and rituals. We are hiding behind our diplomas and degrees. We are hiding behind the glamour and reputation of our religious buildings and organizations because we mistakenly think that God still lives inside temples made by the hands of man. Nevertheless, God is still calling out, "Onward Christian solider, marching as to war, with the cross of Jesus going on before."

God is calling out to the church members. However, we are hiding. We are hiding because we are scared that someone will call us religious fanatics. We are hiding because we think no one will listen to us. We are hiding because we think that we can serve and worship God inside a temple made by the hands of men. Nevertheless, God is calling, “Go, and tell it on the mountain, over the hills and everywhere. Go tell it on the mountain that Jesus, the Christ is born."

God is calling out to the unsaved, but we are hiding. We are more concerned with tires and rims than diapers and food. We are physically present in our homes, but we are no more than a hump on the couch. We are present in our communities, but we are no more than a bump on the highway of life. Nevertheless, God still calls out, “Come ye disconsolate, wherever you languish. Come to the mercy seat and fervently kneel. Bring your wounded hearts; tell your anguish, earth has no sorrow that heaven can not heal."

God is calling out to our country and nation, but we are hiding. We are hiding because we have listened to, agreed with, and acting like Lucifer. We no longer protect God’s creation. We try our best to destroy them. We no longer trust in God. We have Buddha and the psychic hotline instead. Nevertheless, God is still calling out, " Adam, Adam, where fore art thou, Adam."

Although, Adam and Eve sinned, God still loved them. Although God corrected them, he did not abandon them. Although, the voice of justice demanded for them to die because God said, “For the day you eat of this tree you shall surely die." He gave them great mercy instead. We, too, will continue to receive God’s abundant love in spite of the magnitude of our sins. Although, God will and does discipline us, he has promised to never leave us nor forsake us. Although, the righteous voice of justice calls for us to die because the Scriptures say, "The soul that sins shall surely die." A long time ago, God presented us with His love, grace, and mercy. He wrapped Jesus in swaddling clothes and placed him in a manger. When we had nothing to present to God but our filthy unrighteousness, He sacrificed his only begotten son on a wooden Roman cross. He shed the blood of the only Lamb of God just to wash away our sins and now calls us righteous. Even now, He continually calls out to us, "There is a fountain filled with blood drawn from Emmanuel's veins. And sinners plunge beneath the flood lose all their guilt and stain."

When we hear the merciful voice of God calling us, we must realize that God requires an immediate response. As we continue to walk in this present day civilized wilderness, God calls us to respond in spite of our various turmoils, despairs, or sins. He requires us to respond immediately to his crucial call, " I am thine oh Lord. I have heard thy call as it told thy love to me; and I long to rise in the arms of faith and be closer drawn to thee. Draw me nearer, nearer blessed Lord to the cross where thou have died. Draw me nearer, nearer blessed Lord to Thy precious bleeding side."

Once we hear the call of God, the important question is will we respond. Will we come from behind our denominational church walls and compel the lost to come. Will we get up off our do nothing and start to do something. Will we accept the precious sacrifice made upon the rugged cross at Calvary or will we just continue to hide behind our man made temples and tremble because we are afraid that God and the world will discover our sin.

A Call To The Church

From the southern most tip of Florida to the northern most point of Maine, from the shores of Virginia, across the great Mid-west plains unto the star-studded coast of California, our nation has built many prisons in hopes of solving the ever-increasing problem of crime, violence and social decay. Nevertheless, it seems like the faster we build; the quicker they fill. For every criminal that is lock up, two has to be let go. The question that rings in our ears is who is to blame.

Our streets are constantly filled with violence. From the White House to the schoolhouse to the crack house, our people are being gunned down. Our men and women are hooked and obsessed with themselves. Our children watch and listen to violence on television and on the radio, then turn on who ever they can find to act out what they have learned. The question that rings in our ears is who is to blame.

Parents are killing their children and children are killing their parents. We put pressure on our elected officials in hopes of solving our escalating problems. Nevertheless, the crisis continues. We spend endless amounts of time, energy, and money conducting one survey after another in hope of finding the answer to our ever-increasing problems. Yet, we still do not know whom to blame.

Some try to blame God for our problems. After all, He is to one who made man. Nevertheless, He is not the cause of our problems. We place some of the blame on Lucifer, the fallen archangel of God. After all, he did talk man into sinning. Nevertheless, he is not the reason for our problems. In our quest to find someone to pin the blame on, we must realize that the problem and the blame lie only with us. We are to blame for the way our society has become. We are to blame because we have turned away from the ways of God. We have been doing things anyway, we see fit. Because of this, man is to blame.

My brothers and sisters, I stand here today to tell you that I charge humankind. I charge us of being the greatest murderers on the face of the earth. I charge us of being the greatest destroyers. I charge us of being the greatest liars, and the greatest thief on the face of the earth. There is not much good that can be said about the human race, because everywhere we go we create destruction and havoc. Therefore, I charge us.

Furthermore, we are guilty as charged. We are guilty as charged because the evidence is before us. The evidence is in our prisons. The evidence is in our homes. The evidence is in our schools and in our churches. Because of the path we have chosen to take, we have brought disease, crime, and destruction into our communities. Murder, rape, and homosexuality have become common in our lives. In spite of what the Word of God says, we do not have a problem with it.

We seek to make a profit off the diseases that has infested our people, by selling them high priced cures that does more harm than good. We sell religion to the masses by wrapping it and calling It Television Evangelism. We seek to justify murder, by making abortions legal. We have tried to change what God has called sin by calling it an alternative lifestyle. However, there is a price to pay. That price is the many problems we now face. This is why we are to blame.

However, there is hope. Amid the boiling stew pot of international strife, confusion, and rebellion, beyond the smog-covered turmoil of urban violence, corruption, and social decay, there is a fresh breeze blowing. It is a breeze capable of cooling the stew and blowing away the smog. Something exciting is happening to the churches around the country. Like the rushing mighty wind, whose sound filled the church at Pentecost, this something is a breeze that reverberates as surely as it refreshes.

This breeze is the Holy Spirit of God. He is filling people with insight as well as inspiration, blessings and power. He is the Spirit of wisdom and revelation that not only inspired the writings of the Holy Scriptures but also breathed insight into the wisdom of the Word of God. Upon receiving this power, the church is commissioned to deliver the gospel of Jesus to the streets to the hurt and lost. For too long, we have sat still and watched as the unholy angels of Lucifer brought drugs, violence, and moral decay to our front door. Now, it is time for us to stand up and say loudly, we will not take it anymore.

Each day, drugs, alcohol, illicit sex, and spiritual captivity have destroyed our loved ones. Each day, they are destroyed because we have allowed the very moral fiber of this great country to be torn to pieces by our enemy. Each day, our government spends our tax dollars to build more prisons and institute more programs to get our fellow citizens off drugs and to get our children to act right. However, when we accurately look at the figures, we discover that the more we spend the worse the problem gets.

The solution to our problems is not in the money that we spend or the programs that we institute. The solution lies in the gift that God has given to the world. This gift is His church and the spiritual authority that we possess. As saved children of God, we have already experienced Jesus' love in our lives and know the ability of God to change us. Now it is time for us to take this knowledge and use it to save our country. We can take this country and turn it back to God, if we just get up out of our seats and get to work.

Paul writes in Colossians 1: 12-14, 'Giving thanks to unto the father, who has enabled you to share in the inheritance of the saints in the light. He has rescued us from the power of darkness and transferred us into the Kingdom of His beloved Son, in whom we have redemption and the forgiveness of sin.' Paul did not say will rescue us, as in the future, rather he said God has rescued us from the power of the darkness.

God has rescued or freed us from the power and authority of Lucifer. He has given us the power to defeat the already defeated enemy. If we use this authority, we can take back our children. If we use this authority, we can take back our spouses. If we use this authority, we can take back our homes. If we use this authority, we can take back our communities. If we use this authority, we can take our cities and our country from the grip of Lucifer.

We can do it. We can fight the good fight of faith and take our loved ones from Lucifer. However, we cannot do it sitting behind the four walls of our church buildings. We must go into the streets. We must go into the jailhouse. We must seek and save those that are lost. This is why God gave us the Holy Spirit. The Holy Spirit empowers us to do the work that Jesus commissioned us to do. That is to go into the whole world and make disciples. We can do it because Jesus has given us the authority over our enemies that try to keep us bound in sin. We can do it because Jesus has given us the promise that anything that we ask in His name that too will the Father also do. We can do it because it is our right to do it because we are the saved children of the most high God. We can do it because it must be done.

Paul says in Romans 10: 8-13, "The word is nigh thee, in thy mouth, and in thy heart: that is, the word of faith, which we preach. Because if thou shall confess with thy mouth Jesus is Lord, and shall believe in thy heart that God raised him from the dead, thou shall be saved: for with the heart man believeth unto righteousness; and with the mouth, confession is made unto salvation. For the scripture says, whosoever believeth on Him shall not be put to shame. For there is no distinction between Jew and Greek: for the same Lord is Lord of all, and is rich unto all that call upon him: for, whosoever shall call upon the name of the Lord shall be saved." If we want to free our loved ones, we must introduce them to Jesus. If we want to save our country, we must introduce them to Jesus. We must get them to understand that Jesus is the only answer to the problems we face. Jesus is the only solution to the overcrowded prisons. Jesus is the only solution for the violence in our streets. We must introduce Jesus in order to solve our problems.

God is looking for people that are in love with him and that want to see people saved regardless of race, creed, color, social standing, or economic status. God is looking for people that are willing to venture outside the confinement of the four walls of the local church to do what He commissioned them to do. This is the reason God built the house we call church.

God built His church to seek and save His lost children. In order for us, His saved children to do this, we must transcend beyond the limited thinking that was introduced to us in our upbringing. We must transcend beyond the limited theological thinking that are being taught to us in our denominational churches. We must come to realize that heaven is not a denominational place. We must come to realize that God is not a denominational God. Even though, we are denominational people, we must not and cannot allow our denominations to hinder us from being apart of the church that God built.

We have been called by Jesus to carry His saving Gospel to the lost wherever we can find them. We are ministers to those Lucifer and his unholy agents have trapped into a life of sin. We must evangelize the communities that we live in and reap the harvest. We must venture out into the streets and knock on doors. We must witness to people in stores and in our workplace. We need to persuade them to make Jesus their lord and savior. We must teach them about the Word of God. We must introduce them to the church that God built.

The church that God built is made up of all people regardless of the denominations. The church that God built is constructed for all people regardless of the color of their skin or the nation of their origin. The church that God built is not made to separate man from man. The church that God built is created to reconcile man to God and then man to man. Nevertheless, most of, if not all of our denominations are endeavoring to rebuild those same walls that the blood of Jesus eliminated. Nevertheless, the children of God must stand differently because we are the church that God built.

We stand differently because we cannot afford to stand behind any wall that separates us from our lost and hurting brothers and sisters. We stand differently because we cannot stand behind walls of denominationalism, cultural superiority, racial prejudice, and erroneous ideologies. We stand differently because we realize that God has created us as new creatures. We stand differently because we realize that God does not call us African American, White American, Hispanic American, Japanese, or Asian Christians. He has labeled us as the saved children of God and placed on us a royal and powerful inheritance. God has placed us in the church that He built.

We stand differently and we stand proudly because we are called to stand for the very things that Jesus died for. We are called to stand for treating everyone with love, kindness, and care. We are call to stand for peace, hope, and charity. We are called to lay down our lives so our fallen brothers and sisters may be lifted up to God. We are called to stand for Christ. This is why we are different, and this is who we are. We are just men and women that are totally in love with God. We are men and women who stand for Jesus, the Christ because we are the church that God built.

The church that God built believes that all men and women are sinners and have been or can be saved by the grace of God. The church that God built believes that the great commission is the first and most important mission statement of God's church. The church that God built believes that Jesus is coming back for His church. The church that God built believes in everything in the Holy Bible from Genesis to Revelations. The church that God built does not compromise on the doctrinal belief set forth in the Holy Bible. The church that God built main concern is getting our unsaved brothers and sisters into the church that God built.

The church that God built is the only hope for the world. We are the solution God gave to the world. We must come out of hiding and get to work. Paul continues in Romans 10: 14-15, 'How then shall they call on Him in whom they have not believed? How shall they believe in Him whom they have not heard? How shall they hear without a preacher? And how shall they preach, except they be sent?' We have been sent to deliver the answer to the problems of our country. We are their only hope. We must deliver the good news.

We must give the good news to our lost and hurting brothers and sisters. We must tell them of our unique kinship. We must tell them that they have been place outside of the church that God built because of their unrepented sins. We must tell them that this will not stop them from becoming the saved children of God. We must tell them the only way for them to get in the church that God built is for them to believe in Jesus.

We must give them the good news that God want to make them a part of the church that He built. We must tell them to, 'Come to Jesus. He can save you.' We must tell them to, 'Come to Jesus. He can heal you.' We must tell them to, 'Come to Jesus. He will forgive you.' We must tell them to, 'Come to Jesus, just now.' If we tell them, they will come but we must tell them. We must get out our seats; we must come out of the four walls of the church building and we must tell them and bring them to the church that God built.

Three Crisis Three Solutions One answer

The United States of America is a very diverse and well-educated country. There are countless institutions of higher learning in America. Yet, in spite of this vast number of schools and colleges, some Americans still do not meet the intellectual standards of the rest of the nation. They do not meet these intellectual standards because they have not applied what was taught to them. Intellect is more than the ability to know a large amount of information. Intellect is also the ability to apply that information you know for the intended purpose.

Nevertheless, one disturbing fact is clear concerning America spiritually as a people and a nation. Although, we invest our time, energy, and money into our religion and personal beliefs, the average church member has no personal knowledge of God other than what has been told to them on Sunday morning. The fact is as a country, a people, and a nation, America really is spiritually illiterate.

The reason for this lack of spiritual intellect could be as the children of El Elyon, the most high God; we do not have much of a dialogue with God. Moses and Elijah had dialogue with God in a visible and audible form. However, all we have are the common memorizes prayers and our visits to our church buildings. Nevertheless, the real underlying cause of our spiritual illiteracy is in our comprehension and understanding of what the Scriptures has to say to us as present day Christians.

Realistically, since each person comprehends what they hear, see, and read differently from the next person, it is hard for our pastors, teachers, and preachers to get the entire congregation to comprehend and understand what is being communicated from God. Communication is not just, what is being said by the speaker; communication is also, what is being comprehended and understood by the listener.

However, in order to hear, comprehend, and understand what the Spirit of God is saying to the church that God calls the body of Christ, we must hear from the Scriptures our place, position, and stand as the children of El Elyon, the most high God. By not knowing these things, we have developed into a nation that is still struggling with knowing whose we are.

This question is constantly being asked in our music, our books, and television programs we watch. In America, we classify ourselves by our race, our income, our political affiliations, and our religious denomination. In America, we never know whom we will see in the mirrors of reality because we are obsessed with changing reality and ourselves.

We tend to measure or identify ourselves according to our success, our friends, and our degrees. In our society, our self worth is tied to our stock portfolios, our trips to exotic locations, and investments in our personal properties. Shamefully, we have allowed ourselves to be fooled into thinking that is what life is all about; we have been told that what counts the most is how many toys and joys of life you have before you die.

Moreover, this same lie has found its way into our homes. In our homes, we define ourselves according to the things we purchase because some voice on the radio or television told us and because the newspaper gave us a so-called coupon to use. Dr. this and, Dr. that, among many others tells us how we should feel, act, and think because we think we cannot think for ourselves. In our homes, Neumann Marcus, Vanity Fair, or the latest Cover Girl models tell us how much we should weigh, eat, and drink. Sadly, we listen and we do.

Moreover, the modern day denominations and church buildings have embraced this same ideology. Our denominations measure themselves by the size of its buildings, the wealth, and power of its congregations, and the prestige and political influence of its leaders. Those of us who become members of these church buildings measure the church itself by the amount of members, the entertainment, and the work we can pay someone to do for us.

As great as our accomplishments are, they cannot hide the fact that we really do not know who we are. By not knowing and understanding who we are, we have become double-minded Christians. By not knowing and understanding who we are, we will miss the mark of being the church without a spot or wrinkle. Contrary to popular opinion, God did not save us so we can play dress up on Sunday morning and parade around in our denominational tombs and monument.

The true church does not exist because of our traditions, ceremonies, or organization founders. We exist, we move, and we are who we are because God has a message to deliver. We are who we are because Jesus, the Christ died on the cross to buy our soul from our old master. We have been bought with a high price and that make us who we are. We are here to tell the rest of this racially divided, emotionally scared, and spiritually insecure world that they too have been bought with a high price. Their sin debt has been paid in full. Because of the shedding of the Blood on Calvary, we all can become the children of El Elyon. This is why we were saved. We were saved to do the work God sets before us because we belong to El Elyon, the most high God.

The Scriptures, which is the doctrine of Christ, is the foundation that our faith is built on; the truths that are contained on the pages are our life and our hope. The Scriptures informs us of the ways of God and directs us to the pathways of God. Therefore, we must stand on our faith in God according to what is written in the Scriptures. This belief or spiritual stand is the reason God calls us to be more than conquers. This stand is why when sickness and trials come; we can know and understand that all things work together for the good of those who love the Lord and who are called according to God purpose. The stand that we are to take as the children of God is right where the Scriptures instruct us to stand. This is because, without the Scriptures, all of our hope of salvation dies.

However, because of the truths found in the Scriptures, we stand and remain strong because we are anchored to the rock of God. In times of trouble and trials, we stand because we are anchored. In times of temptation, we stand and remain strong because we are anchored. Even when we fall, we can get up and stand strong because we are anchored. We are anchored to the rock of El Elyon and we have the power and presence of the Holy Spirit to keep us on our feet. Therefore, we stand and we stand right where the Scriptures tell us because we stand for God.

However, the average church members have not decided where to stand. We have allowed the trappings of life and the lust for prosperity to compromise our stand. Instead of going with God, we go with the tide of public opinion and hope for the best. We no longer stand with or for God. We stand with our church-going politicians, movie stars, and religious celebrities. However, we should read the Scriptures for ourselves and let the Holy Spirit guide us into all truth and understanding.

We grievously contribute our hard-earned wages to their financial coffers because we have been deceived into believing that we must go through someone else to get to God. Our Christian-elected presidents and politicians say that it is okay to kill, destroy, steal, and fight wars, and we stand behind that. We stand there because we have decided to be good little deceived American church members. Nevertheless, in reality, we have allowed Lucifer to fool us into getting back into the same muck and mire God rescued us from.

The reason for our current spiritual crisis is we do not know whose we are and because of that, we do not know where to stand. As the children of El Elyon, we stand on the information found in the Scriptures. We stand for the things of God. We stand for love, mercy, peace, and righteousness, because Jesus stood on the cross for us. We stand for these things because we cannot afford to stand anywhere else. We know and understand that our salvation depends upon our stand. We have the intellect to act upon this knowledge because the salvation of those not yet saved depends upon our actions.

According to the Scriptures, we are enabled to stand by experiencing God's Spirit, mercy, grace, power, and love. When we stand on our spiritual feet right where we live, we can help someone else to stand. In doing this, we will be following the examples and instructions of Jesus and the disciples. According to the Scriptures, we are to have the mind of Jesus, the Christ. We are instructed to be in this present age but not to be of this present age. We are instructed to forsake everything and follow Jesus, the Christ.

We hear and read that God so loved this racially divided, emotionally scared, and spiritually insecure world so much that God sent his only son to die for what we had done. We are commanded to be steadfast and firm in our belief and faith in God. We are expected to be unmovable in our hope in and expectation of God. Therefore, because we are the children of El Elyon, we abound in the works of God. We are empowered by His Spirit and we are capable to do the work. We are the body of Christ. We might be lambs among wolves, but God made us to take over.

We are to heal the sick, cast out demons, and raise the dead of our society. We are the children of El Elyon. God has put us back together after sin had torn us asunder. He has reshaped us by the Word of God and the Holy Spirit. He reveals to us through the Scriptures that we are the very image and likeness of God. The Holy Spirit of God transforms us into the righteousness of God. He teaches us the ways, concepts, and percepts of God. He stands us on our spiritual feet as the children of El Elyon. We are packed with the power of God. We are a force to be reckoned with.

Therefore we stand. We stand not because of our denomination, or church building. We stand not for our country, the system, or the people we chose to run things. We stand only because one day Jesus, the Christ stood for us. We stand because God has given us the Holy Spirit. We stand because by His Spirit we live, move and exist.

Nevertheless, we tend to think that our education, wealth, and religion can help us to stand. We see the results. The results are we live in a world plagued by trouble and violence. The results are a nation on the verge of spiritual bankruptcy. We have allowed the false prophets of our society to lead us astray. The results are a nation, a church, and a people in crisis because we do not know our place, position, and stand as the children of El Elyon, the most high God.

In our zeal to fool ourselves, we discovered three things to solve the problem that plague our society. In our quest to make a stand in this mad, psychopathic jungle, we have produced more educated people than most of the world. We can learn online at home or at a vast number of community colleges. If we desire the college experience,

our government, our jobs, and a host of private foundations are willing to send us to any number of institutions of higher learning. Because of our drive to know more, America has increased the standard of living in our country and across the world.
Our educated society has brought advantages and advances that were only a dream to our forefathers. Nevertheless, we still do not know how to solve the nightmares we face each day. Education teaches us that together we can stand, but it does not give us the power it takes to stand. Education has taught us the history, the failures, and the achievements of our people. Nevertheless, it has not stopped racism, poverty, war, or oppression. Education is good, but education is not God.

America has become a prosperous and powerful society because of our constant drive to educate the masses. The average household income has gone from $7,000 in 1964 to around $35,000 today. America produces and or sells most of the consumable goods in the world. Our capitalist ideology allows us to lend money to the world and profit off others miseries. Our calling card is bring us your tired, your hungry, and your huddled masses and our lotteries, casinos and good old American greed will turn them in to millionaires overnight. America is truly a wealthy nation because we have the Midas touch.

Nevertheless, we enjoy life much less than before. We work two jobs so we can live like someone else. We go home too tired and too deep in debt to enjoy the house or those in it. We rob and steal from each other and will kill anyone who gets in our way to the top. America is wealthy and wealth is good. However, in spite of what we stamp on our money, wealth is not God.

One of the main principles this great country is built upon is the freedom to worship any god we want. We worship when we want, where we want, and what we want. It is apart of our Constitution. In America, we do not force religion on people like in a Muslim country. In America, we can freely choose the religion we want. Consequently, we can choose not to believe in anything, not even ourselves.

This benefit has made America great and strong. We are the melting pot for all races and cultures. Consequently, we have become a country that worships any god. To paraphrase, Paul in Acts 17:22, "People of America, I see that in every way you are very religious." However, because of our much-prized religious freedom, the body of Christ has become many different and useless denominations. America is now overrun with false prophets preaching false doctrine, because America is a nation that will serve any god. Religion is good, but religion is not God.

Therefore, this leads us to the only solution to the crisis we face. The answer is Jesus, the Christ. He is our Lord and the head of the Body of Christ. He has given us our commission. The Holy Spirit of God is inside us to enable us. Nevertheless, what are we doing? We are building temples with our hands when God has said he will not live in them. We have Holy Ghost parties and jump and shout about Jesus, but never invite the Holy Spirit of God to come in our lives. We chase behind the American dream and our piece of the pie in the sky and have left those lost in sins to save themselves.

We let our underpaid preachers, pastors, and teachers study the Scriptures for us, because we are to busy. We tune in to our favorite television prophet to tell us just what we want to hear. We pay our religious organizations to do the work God assigned to our hands. We chase after our dreams five, six and seven days a week, but only allow three hours on Sunday to hear from God. Therefore, the crisis we face is a vivid and loud indicator that we have gone wrong somewhere.

Something is wrong when raising money and erecting buildings become more important than saving souls. Something is wrong when we refuse to go out and harvest because someone might call us bible-toting, religious fanatics. Something is wrong when we call sin acceptable and homosexuality a right. Something is wrong because we, the present day children of God, have sat down on the job. God will turn us over to a reprobate mind. We sing with our mouths that we love the Lord, but our hearts are far from Him. We are not really singing the song; we are just mouthing the words. The question we, present day children of God need to hear is, as Thomas Shepherd writes, "Must Jesus bear the cross alone and all this world go free. No, there is a cross for everyone and there is a cross for me." As the body of Christ, we need to hear the words we sing because they really do mean something. They mean that we are the one child of El Elyon to stand up in the midst of a cowering world and respond, "The consecrated cross I'll bear till death shall set me free and then go home my crown to wear for there is a crown for me." We stand and we do these things because we know our place, position, and stand. We stand for God.

PROBLEM PURPOSE PLAN SOLUTION

From the view of the outside world, the defeat and exile of the Jewish race demonstrated the failure of their God. It exhibited to the Gentiles that the Jewish religion was without foundation. The Israelites were so discredited by their defeat that the surrounding nations said that it was foolish for them to continue to remain loyal to God. Today, the people of the world are judging the Christian religion in the court of public opinion and we have been pronounced useless and out of date.

The church has not solved the many problems that plague our society so the world views our ideas as old fashion, our services as boring, and our God as dead. Due to the facts we are presented with, we cannot deny the accusations. However, the answers to the world's problems cannot be found in theology, ideology, or denominational doctrine. Since the problem is the sins of the people of the world and of the church, the answer can only be found with God. Moreover, we must realize that His divine plan has not completely manifested itself. {Read Ezekiel 36: 16-23}

The sins of the people of the world and God's own people are the reason we are plague with our current problems. Sin, in this day, has been greatly distorted and our hearts have been dulled to the sad effect of it. We still recognize the sins of stealing, killing, and slandering. However, according to the way that the world and some Christians think, it is acceptable to commit adultery, engage in homosexual relationships, or even practice idol worship. We say it is acceptable as long as we are not caught or no one is offended. However, when we sin, people do get hurt and all sin offends God.

Sin is the root cause of all of our problems that we face as a society. Sin not only causes problems for us, it also causes problems for God. God is holy and He will not tolerate sin. He considers it an act of rebellion and a declaration of war. It hurts God when we chose to sin the same as it hurts a parent when their child chooses to be disobedient. Just as a parent must disciple the disobedient child, God must discipline us for our sins. God cannot and will not condone or ignore our sins. His anger erupts against us when we sin and ignore the truth about Him. When the day comes for God to judge us for our sins, no excuses will be accepted.

Romans 1: 18-20 tells us God has revealed Himself plainly to all people through His creation. God has revealed to us what He is like; nevertheless, we chose to reject even this basic knowledge. God has given us an inner sense of His requirements, a sense of morals; still we chose not to live up to them. We know the truth. It has been put on the inside of us. It has been written down for us in a language we can understand. Moreover, we will bring down the wrath of God if we continue to ignore it. Realize, when we chose to ignore God and remain in our sins, it makes us unacceptable to God. Regardless of what we try to do to solve the world's problems, not even God can solve them because of our sins.

God created us to be in control of this world. Because of our sins, we cannot be the kind of people that He created us to be. However, our sins do not stop God from being God. In spite of our sins, God is still in control. In spite of our sins, God still does not want us to perish in Hell's flames. In spite of our sins, God will fulfill His promise to make Abraham descendants as numerous as the stars in the night sky and as uncountable as the sands on the seashore. In spite of our sins, God still says that we can be saved. In Joel 2:32, He says, "And everyone that calls upon the name of the Lord will be saved." This is the purpose of God. His purpose is to save us because to ourselves we are a lost cause. First, we need to renounce our sins and ask Him to save us. {Read Ezekiel 36:24}

God's plan for our salvation is foretold more than once in the Word of God. It is a detailed plan, but it is easy to understand. This simple plan starts with a necessary search and rescue mission. In verse 24, we are shown how God will conduct this mission. He says, 'I will take you out of the nations,' and 'I will gather you from all countries.' God is searching for those He wants to bless. God is looking for those that want to be blessed. He is searching in the crack houses and whorehouse. God is searching every street, every corner, and every valley. No matter what condition He finds them in, he will rescue them. He will search them out and bring them back to their own land. He will search for us and bring us back to where we belong. God will bring us back to Himself. {Read Ezekiel 36:25}

After the search and rescue mission, God will cleanse them of their sins. There is a story of a young man that was given some land by his grandfather. At first, this piece of property looked as if it was worthless because of the vast forest and thick undergrowth. The young man complained about the land until someone informed him that he could make some money off the trees. The young man went to work cutting the trees and took them to the sawmill. As he continued to cut, he came upon some large rocks. He picked up one of the rocks, looked at it, and saw something shining in the sunlight. Then, he started cleaning the dirt and mud off it. After a period of cleaning, the young man found the rock to be solid gold. {Read Ezekiel 36:25}

We, too, are found to be priceless treasures after God cleanses us of our sins. In the sinful conditions we are in, the world quickly judges us another piece of worthless moving dirt. We are seen this way because the world cannot see through the muck and mire of our sins. They cannot see through the forest of hopelessness and despair. They cannot see past the thick undergrowth of our addictions and habits. Nevertheless, our God can. He looks past our faults and He sees our needs.

Once He sees our sins, He uses what the world cannot understand and He cleanses us from all our sins and unrighteousness. Robert Lowery writes, “What can wash away my sins, nothing but the blood of Jesus. What can make me whole again, nothing but the blood of Jesus? O', how precious is that flow that makes me white as snow. No other fount I know nothing but the blood of Jesus." God cleanses us with this spiritual water, because physical water can never remove the sin. God cleanses us spiritually because physical cleaning is not enough. Physical cleaning takes care of only the outside, but God wants us clean on the inside where sin does the most damage. {Read Ezekiel 36:25-26}

God will cleanse us from all of our impurities. He takes away the things that make us unholy and impure. He removes the demons, habits, and our wrong way of thinking. God will cleanse us from our idols. He takes away the things that cause us to do wrong. He will remove the false gods, the demons, and sometimes-even people. God will cleanse us from everything that separates us from him and that causes us to fall into sin. After the cleansing, God transforms us into what He would have us to be. Sin makes us miss the mark of the high calling of God in Jesus Christ. Sin is our failure to be all that God would have us to be. Sin makes us not be the men and women God created us to be. Sin makes our children not be the children we train them to be. Sin makes us miss the mark of God. {Read Ezekiel 36:27}

Nevertheless, when God find us in the wilderness of sin, He transforms us into new creations. God takes our uncaring heart and replaces it with a heart that cares. God takes our unloving heart and replaces it with a heart that loves. God removes our unbelieving heart and gives us a heart that believes. God empowers us to hit the mark. David wrote in Psalms 51:10 "Create in me a clean heart and renew in me the right spirit." Then in Psalms 51:12 "restore unto me the joy of thy salvation and grant me a willing spirit to sustain me." Without the Spirit of God, we do not have the type of faith it takes to please Him. Without the Spirit of God, we cannot do the thing it takes to please Him. Without the Spirit of God, we will miss the mark and will lift up our eyes from Hell. {Read Ezekiel 36:28}

The next step in God's plan of salvation is restoration. God has promised to restore us. No matter how impure our lives are because of sin, God offers us a fresh start. God will restore us as His people and save us from our sins. God will restore us from the disgrace of our sins. God will restore us, not by the things that we do, nor by the songs that we sing. God will store us by His grace. The songwriter writes, "Amazing Grace, how sweet the sound that saved a wrench like me." This is what God will use to restore us. He will use nothing but the Grace of God. {Read Ezekiel 36: 29-37}

After the restoration, God will resettle us into the promises of His covenant. Because of our sins, we cannot lay claim to the promises God has given us in the New Covenant. However, through the process of His divine plan of salvation, God will restore us to those promises. {Read Ezekiel 36:38}

The final process of His plan of salvation is recognition. This is not recognition for anything we have done. Although God will make us new creations, this is not recognition for anything we have become. This is recognition of who God is. The Word of God says in verse 38, "Then, they will know that I am God." The world, that once saw us as outcast, dirty, and diseased, will see us as new and changed creatures because of God's work in us.

Because of this glorious transformation, they will declare that truly He is God. Our testimony will be great, because God is great. The song we sing, will be, "What a mighty God we serve. Heaven and earth adore Him, the angel bow before Him. What a mighty God we serve."

Why did God save us?

One of the most exciting things to experience is someone accepting Christ into their lives. During this developing or growing stage, the newborn child of God sense something meaningful has happened to them. They desire to change their lives and strive to become better persons. Nevertheless, somewhere between the excitement and the desire, the importance of our salvation escapes us and we fail to mature and become the men and women of God we were recreated to become.

This all too real threat of not growing in our relationship with God should cause us to reflect and ask questions about the real purpose and meaning of our salvation. We must seek to understand what we have done spiritually as well as physically when we step forward to accept God's offer of salvation. We must understand what we are to do, become, and what do we receive because of our obedience, baptism, and salvation. These questions will only be answered by reading and mediating on the Scriptures and through the teachings of the Holy Spirit of God.

According to the Scriptures, upon our salvation, we are reborn or recreated as the children of God. However, our rebirth does not involve our physical appearance. This stage of our recreation involves only our spiritual man. Before salvation, we are spiritually dead to God because of our many sins. Because of this, we needed to be reborn or recreated spiritually. We needed to be reunited and put in line with God and his will for us. Therefore, when we accepted God's offer of salvation and go through the physical ritual of baptism, we die and are buried to our old spiritual self, and rise in a new spiritual relationship with God.

II Corinthians 5:17 informs us that old things pass away and everything becomes new. The old ideal of sin is replaced with the new ideal of living righteous because of God. We replace those old ideals and thoughts with the information we receive from studying the Scriptures. We receive instructions and revelations by meditating on what the Holy Spirit of God teach us. The Scriptures informs us that sin made us enemies with God, but Jesus still died for our sake. He did this to make us friends with God. Sin once stood between God and us, but now nothing can ever separate us from His love.

Therefore, as we continue to read the Scriptures and respond to the teachings of the Holy Spirit of God, we will be empowered to do the will of God. This is the stage where the spiritual recreation joins with the physical recreation to make us everything that God needs us to be for Him. James 1:18 states that God gives us the rebirth through the Scriptures and it renews our minds when we read it. The spiritual rebirth has nothing to do with our efforts or us, but the physical rebirth is all about our efforts. God gives us His understanding, wisdom, and gifts by the teachings of the Holy Spirit. God then empowers us to do what He has taught us. As we allow the Holy Spirit of God to lead us, we mature in and develop our relationship to God.

According to Titus 3: 5-7, we are not saved because of any of the righteous things we do. God saved us just because He loved us. He had mercy on us because of Jesus birth, life, and eventual death on the cross. Then God recreated us spiritually through the Holy Spirit of God. Because of this, we are no longer enemies of God. We have been accepted into the family of God and are now co-heirs with Christ to the kingdom of God.

Nevertheless, the process of renewal and maturing into men and women of God is a continual journey. As we actively work out our salvation by doing what God instructs us to, we are made into the image and likeness of God. II Corinthians tells us to renew our minds daily. In John 5: 24-25, we are informed that when we hear God's words and believe that God has, is, and will do what he promised, we will be saved. The book of Romans states that faith comes by hearing and hearing by the Word of God. Therefore, we are made alive in God by our belief in what the Scriptures has revealed to us and the Holy Spirit of God has taught us.

Ezekiel 18:4 states the soul that sins will surely die. As the child of God, we understand that if we are in sin, we are separated from God. Because of sin, we are also dead to the ways of God. When we are in sin, we no longer travel on the path of righteousness. When we are in sin, we are in league with Lucifer. This union will earn us the same reward that is reserved for him. This is the reason the Scriptures tell us to confess our sins to God. God is faithful and just to forgive us of our sins and cleanses us from all unrighteousness. Only God can restore us back into a right relationship with Him.

In sin, we are as good as dead. Nevertheless, because God loves us, we have been given a way out of or a path of escape from the wages of sin. God has given us the Holy Spirit to guide us along the path of righteousness. The Holy Spirit of God teaches us about God and the things of God. When we live in total dependence and complete obedience to God, we mature into the men and women of God and experience the presence of God in our lives.

This path of escape is the information found in Scriptures. God has allowed this information to be proclaimed all over the world. Because of this information, we have turned from the darkness into the light of God. In the light, we have clarity of purpose. In the light, we can discover our position in the body of Christ. We can see those still traveling in the path of darkness and we can point them to the light.

During our pointing of others to the road of salvation, we began to develop or mature in our relationship with God. The more we proclaim the good news to our brothers and sisters, the more we hear the Word of God, ourselves. We are not told just make disciples. We are instructed to teach them everything we have been taught. Therefore, the more we teach them, the more God will reveal to us to teach to them. That is good news. The good news is God has decided to take nobodies and recreate us into His image and likeness. He has placed us as his royal priest. He calls us a holy nation; He has made us heirs to his kingdom.

This is the will of God for our lives. God's will is for us to experience His presence. Through doing the things that we are instructed to do in the Scriptures, we experience the presence of God. Because of this presence, we have unspeakable joy. We are unshakable in our belief in God. We experience unexplainable peace.

Because of this, we are thankful to God. He claimed us, although we did not know him. He claimed us and he recreated us into his image and likeness. He claimed us and called us to be peculiar people. We are thankful because God has chosen to bless us with more than we can every dare to ask for. We are thankful because we are experiencing more of the wonderful Presence of God. We are thankful because he has chosen to write our names in the Lambs Book of Life.

However, now that God has chosen us, we must now choose him. We must choose to follow the teachings of Jesus as revealed in the Scriptures. We must choose God regardless of what the world may say, think, or invent. Therefore, by our obedience, we choose God. We choose him when we go into the highways and byways and compel the lost to come to God. When we choose God, He will empower us to do His work.

The Power of God is inside us.

As a child of God, we grow and transform into the image and likeness of God. We are given the indwelling presence of the Holy Spirit of God. Truthfully, we belong to God. However, we do not belong to God just because he made us. We belong to God because we chose to put our faith and trust in what he has already provided for our salvation. We belong only to God. We are called his special children. We live and walk by faith. We believe that God is. We are the redeemed of God. We are set aside for the Holy Spirit of God to empower us to do the works of God.

Nevertheless, being a child of God is not one of the easiest jobs. We are called to live opposite to the world. We are taught that the world's way of existing does not lead to righteousness. A child of God is often looked upon as peculiar because we are not guided by the same set of principals as the rest of the world. The world constantly denies the ways of righteousness. The world constantly presents a struggle for the child of God. Nevertheless, in the midst of this struggle to stand, we are empowered with the presence of God to stand us on our feet.

When we study the Scriptures and allow the Holy Spirit to teach us, the forces of God is revealed to us. We are not in this struggle alone. Our help comes from God. Therefore, nothing should keep us from doing what God has recreated us to do. The Scriptures teaches us that God has always come to the aid of His people. God empowered Abraham to rescue Lot. God empowered Moses to lead Israel out of Egypt. The Scriptures teaches us that God has promised this same help to us. God will be a constant help in times of trouble. Nevertheless, we must choose to remain faithful and obedient to Him.

The only way the Holy Spirit can work in our lives is through our faithful obedience to God. 1st Peter 1:5 tell us that God has shielded us by His power and empowers us to become all God has in store for us. Romans 8:31 states 'If God be for us who can be against us.' Therefore, because of our faithful obedience to God, we are empowered by him.

Moreover, the empowering presence of the Holy Spirit of God continues to build or form us in our position as the children of God. As we study and meditate upon the Scriptures, the Holy Spirit of God guides us and forms us into the body of Christ or the Church. We are empowered with real power. This same power was in Jesus. We are given this power so we can do the works of God.

We are more than conquerors. We can do all things through Christ who strengthens us. Because of our love and the presence of the Holy Spirit, all things work together for our good according to God's purpose. As we grow and continue to mature in our relationship with and to God, we develop into powerful men and women of God that study and mediate on the Scriptures daily. We study to find information about God. We study to find out information on what God has done for us. We study to understand the nature of God's power and to uncover the purpose for it. We study to understand why we need God's power. Foremost, we study to understand how God wants us to use His power.

Our need to know these things is instrumental in our development from the children of God into the men and women of God. Ephesians 6 states, 'our fight is not against flesh and blood.' Our enemy is Lucifer and the millions of unholy spirits, principalities, powers, and evil forces. Our enemies are also those that are under his influence. The children of God face a real and active force each day. These forces are destined to draw us off the path of righteousness. Lucifer, a fallen angel made by God, leads these forces. God made him and empowered him.

However, his pride got him exiled from heaven. Regardless, Lucifer did not stop being an angel. He can be a snake, act like a lion, or appear as an angel of light. Lucifer is the father of all lies. He tries to deceive us any way he can. His purpose is to deceive and accuse the brethren. His strategy is to steal our attention in order to get us off the path of righteousness. He desires to destroy any chance of us growing up in our relationship to God. He wants to kill us before we can mature into the mighty men and women of God.

As we mature into the men and women of God, we are equipped and empowered to battle the enemy. We are able to see the traps and snares that are set for us. Because of the indwelling Holy Spirit of God, we see them and we do not stumble. The Scriptures tells us to be aware because false doctrine and fake teachers will try to seduce us. We are warned about becoming lukewarm in our attitude toward God. If we are found in sin, God will remove us from His kingdom. If we start to care more for the world, than for God, we will become undesirable to Him. The enemy put many traps and snares along the pathway to trip us up. As the mature men and women of God, we must rely on the Scriptures and the Holy Spirit of God to guide us. We are given a way out of every trial and temptation. We are the mighty men and women of God. We are empowered by God to overcome and conquer the enemy.

Therefore, we must understand the gifts of the powerful presence of the Holy Spirit of God. We must understand the power behind the gifts is God. Lucifer will try to take the very blessings that God gives us and use them against us. He will try to lure us into a false sense of security. We will start to seek after the prosperity and the notoriety of being a child of God. We will start to love the positions and the blessings. Before long, we will be lifting our eyes from Hell. This is why 1st Peter 5: 8 –10 asks us to be sober and watchful. As mature men and women of God, we must remain sober and unaffected by the things around us. We must remain watchful and alert to the movement of the enemy. We are to seek God through the study of the Scriptures. We are to resist Lucifer's attempts to get us off the path of righteousness. Lucifer, the enemy will flee. He will flee because we are able to resist him by the power of the presence of the Holy Spirit of God. The Holy Spirit of God perfects us into the correct image of God. He establishes us in our belief in God. He restores and strengthens us as we continue to mature into the mighty men and women of God.

As the mature men and women of God, we are more concern about our spiritual well being than our material well-being. We are able to stand against the wiles of Lucifer. The men and women of God are completely dependent on God for the strength to stand. We are completely dependent upon God to take care of us. The Scriptures tells us that God will never leave us or forsake us. We believe it. God has promised never to forsake the righteous nor let his seed go begging. We believe it. Because of this belief, God continues to develop us into the body of Christ. When we study the Scriptures, the Holy Spirit of God teaches us the truths of Jesus life, death, and resurrection. The Holy Spirit guards, guides, and instructs us in the ways of God. He helps us to avoid, overcome, and endure everything Lucifer does to make us fall.

The Holy Spirit fits us together with other men and women of God into the Church. We are placed in the church or Body of Christ because we are more than conquerors. Our confidence is not based in the world. We are the mighty men and women of God. We stand confidently for the things of God. We stand for God and He stands with us. Because of our acceptance and the indwelling presence of the Holy Spirit of God, we now stand secure in our relationship with God. We are assured through the

Scriptures that no one can snatch us from the hands of God. We are promised that nothing can separate us from His love. However, this only applies when we remain in our relationship with God. This is the reason we are not to forsake the gathering together with other believers. We are to continue to study and mediate on the Scriptures. Because of this, we will remain strong in our relationship with God. We are told to grid up the loin of our mind. We grow stronger in our relationship with God as we continue to study the Scriptures and allow the Holy Spirit of God to lead us.

We become rooted and grounded in Christ. We are the mighty men and women of God. We must take advantage of every activity that helps us to grow and mature in our relationship with God. We must continue to do the things of God that His Spirit encourages and empowers us to do. Foremost, we must continually examine our walk and ourselves to see where we are in sin. The light of the Holy Spirit will guide us and show us where we need improvement. Once sin is revealed, we confess it and completely trust God to take care of it. Through the indwelling presence of the Holy Spirit of God we are established, strengthen, perfected, settled, and restored into our relationship to and with God. We mature into men and women of God. We are completely dependent and obedient to God. We remain faithful to God because we are the mature men and women of God.

Do you want to find God?

Do you want to find God? Do we want to serve God? Each of us can do this by simply looking for someone less fortunate than we are or even someone more fortunate than we are and pointing him or her to the ROCK that is higher than we are. When we do, we will discover that we are looking at the very image and likeness of God. In this day and time where the influence of Lucifer has gain a great hold on our society, there is need for the children of God to venture outside the confinements of our many church buildings. There is an enormous need for us to go to those Jesus sent us to serve.

However, one of the saddest days in Christian history was the day when even the elect of God became fooled. The elect of God became fooled into thinking that God changed his mind and returned to live in the buildings that we constructed for the purpose of our Sunday meetings. Therefore, we poured our money, time, and attention into the bricks, stones, wood, and mortar that surrounds us for only a few days each week. We hold these man made temples in greater esteem than the temples that God made and the lost souls we see each day.

The real temples of God, mankind, became fooled like Eve by listening to the untrue words of Lucifer. Galatians states that Jesus came to take down the walls that divide us from our fellow man. However, the servants of Lucifer hastened to teach the church of God that it is okay to neglect those lost along the way. They convinced us that God would be more pleased if we gave our tithes and offerings to construct buildings where we could come to worship. Therefore, the sad result is we now care more for a building than we do for the creation of God. If our buildings need something, we quickly sacrifice our time energy and money to provide for its every need. If our buildings calls, we quickly come running and pour upon these false temples of God our attention and care. However, when the real temple of God is hurting and in despair, we shake our heads, point our fingers, and turn the other way. Some of us will sometimes stop and wrongly point the real temple toward the false temple where we worship. We do this because the day have come when even the elect of God has become fooled.

The current state of the body of Christ is not the proper representation intended by God. Jesus did not commission the church of God to venture into the seclusion of an enclosure where only those that join can come. He commissioned us to go into the highways and the byways and compel them to come to the same understanding that the Spirit of God has brought us to. This understanding is simply we are the temple of God because inside of us the Spirit of God forever dwells.

Centuries ago, the apostle Paul loudly declared in Acts 17 that God would not dwell in temples made by the hands of man. Today, the time has come for the church of God to finally heed the words of Paul and understand that God does not dwell in the many edifices, temples, and buildings we have foolishly labeled as the house of God. God is a spirit. God is not and will not be found in buildings made of bricks, stones, wood, and mortar. In the beginning of time, he constructed buildings for him to inhabit. Genesis states that God created man and placed inside man a piece of his spirit. The Scriptures state loudly in Malachi to bring our tithes and offerings into the storehouse so there will be meat in God's house. A storehouse is a place where something is stored. We are the place God has chosen to store His spirit since the beginning of time, therefore we, the human race, are the only storehouse or church of God not a man made building.

However, God is not divided. God is not a Methodist. God is not a Baptist. There is only one God and one church of

God. This church of God is not denominational. However, Lucifer has fooled us into dividing ourselves in spite of the sacrifice Jesus made to bring us together. We have allowed the prophets of Lucifer to fool us into reconstructing the same denominational walls that Jesus died to break down.

There is a popular military tactic called divide and conquer. This is the purpose of denominations. They exist to divide the united body of Christ so Lucifer can conquer our world. If we look around in our communities, it is evident the tactic has worked. The body of Christ is so busy competing against each other that we have forgot the reason we were saved. We have become fooled into thinking that God is all about the denominational agendas we develop. The truth is God is not in our agendas because he has his own agenda. God's agenda is to seek and save the lost. Our denominational agenda is to control this world. God could care less about this world because he has told us he will throw this world and those that cling to it into the lake of fire that is the second death. Therefore, it is our choice to make. We can come together as one body in Christ; or we can be cast into the lake of fire with Lucifer and our denominations. Nevertheless, the time has come to make our choice, because the kingdom of God is at hand.

God is not a respecter of person and with him there is neither Greek nor Jew, bond, nor free. My question is who has bewitched us into separating ourselves into the numerous denominations to which we cling. Denominationalism is not the gospel the disciples preached. They did not preach division of the body of Christ. The disciples spoke of the unity of the believers first with God then with each other. Therefore, since denominations are not the gospel of the disciples, it must be another gospel. Moreover, let anyone that preaches another gospel except the gospel of Christ be damned.

It is important that we realize the truth and turn from the errors of our ways as the people of God. The kingdom of God is at hand and the fields are white and ripe for the harvest. While the world continued to tumble and become engrossed in the abundant sins of our society, the things that mankind once put all of its faith into have been revealed as nothing but a venomous deceitful Ponzi scheme. Our society chased after every thing but the truths and wisdom contained in the word of God. We forgot that the love of money is the root of all evil. Like Eve, our society listened to, agreed with, and decided to act just like Lucifer. The stock market crashed and the global economy failed creating the fiduciary splash felt around the world. Now, the masses are running around like sheep with out a shepherd and the call from God is going forward for the church of God to come out of many and often useless monuments, edifices, and religious buildings. The kingdom of God is at hand and the time has come for the children of God to go to work in the fields of our broken and spiritually bankrupt society. It is time for us to heed the call of God and get to work.

However, here is a necessary look into the reality that now faces each of us. The kingdom of God is at hand and the Master Gardner has returned to examine the fruit of our labor. Like the fig tree in the parable of the unproductive fig tree, God will examine us. Since our work in our society has been left undone, we will be pronounced as unproductive and in sin. The call of God for our destruction will be pronounced because the Scriptures states loudly, 'The soul that sins, it shall surely die.' God will look, see the sin of our undone work, and pronounced 'Cut them down. They are taking up space we can use for something else. However, the love of Christ responded, 'Give them one more chance. I will give them my personal attention for three long years. I will fertilize them with your word. I will bear their sins on the cross. Then, I will fill them with your Holy Spirit. If they produce, it will be fine. If not, then we can cut them down.' The reality is if we are found unproductive, God will cut us down and throw us in to the lake of fire that is the second and final death. This reality comes with the dawning of the end of our days. The kingdom of God is at hand and all questions will soon be answered about the final destination that we have chosen.

However, that destination is determined by the proclamation of our belief. Do we believe in that which even by the magnificent display in nature is but a reality? Do you believe that God has turned our society over to a reprobate mind or are we still of the opinion that our sins will be okay with God? The kingdom of God is at hand and never in the history of mankind has our faith and belief in God been test as it is being tested now. However, we will shiver even harder when we realize of the devastation that faces our society from coast to coast when the Master Gardner returns to check our work.

The kingdom of God is at hand and the shores of our nation are presently plagued with violence, despair, poverty, and shame. These plagues are but the return from the seeds of our past sown upon futile soil. They are the revealing fruit of our national character. Our nation in its infant beginning hurled these seed upon the futile soil of time and history. The pain and suffering that our once prosperous society is enduring is but a small portion of the enormous wage that will be paid. A wage paid for the abundant sins of denial, greed, and disobedience committed by our continuous actions and deeds. These unrighteous proclamations of our true character and belief were made in spite of the righteous words we proclaimed to believe.

The kingdom of God is at hand and the pain and suffer will not end for a very long time. Mother and fathers will continue to cry out from shore to shore as the nation lie dissolute in the waste of the fall of our great economy. It wasted away because we refused to face the truth. The truth is simple and easy to understand. Our documents loudly proclaim in God we trust. The truth is the kingdom of God is at hand and now is the time to let God know exactly where you stand. It is time to stand up. Will you be counted among the workers in the fields? Or will you be line up with the multitude and casted into the lake of fire? The truth is where you spend eternity is your choice.

We fight the good fight, remain faithful, and finish the race

This morning, as I watched the start of a new day, the sun slowly rose over the distant horizon. As the darkness that had previously enveloped the sky quickly and silently retreated to its assigned hiding place, I had to give God his due praise. The night was and is cold and dark. Nevertheless, every day God provides the needed warmth and light to chase the cold darkness away.

As we grudgingly struggle through the hurts of this Christian nightmare of greed and corruption, we are now forced to cast our eyes down into the pit of our coming recession. First, we were jolted by the greed and the corruption in corporate America. Nevertheless, that is corporate America. Greed is expected. We wonder will these nights of chastisement for America end.

However, we never saw the shock waves of this Christian scandal coming. Although, many knights in shining armor have come to the rescue with their money and their knowledge, we now face the chastisement of a looming recession. In a recession, our money will be worth less than an icemaker in Nome Alaska.

Now here are the real questions that need to be addressed. Do we go back to being that same illiterate church going person? Will we just exist spiritually with our heads stuck in the proverbial sand of Christian ignorance? Will we learn from the mistakes of blindly following just anyone that proclaim they are men of God or our savior from our crisis?

Moreover, will we continue to travel down the same path of spiritual trickery that got us here in the first place? Will we continue to blindly believe what someone has to proclaim concerning our soul salvation? Will we simply take time to pick up the bible? Will we finally research and work out our own soul salvation with fear and trembling?

In the mist of all our continuing joy and pending sadness, we must answer these questions. The question that must be answered first and utmost is to which hill or more directly from whom has our help come? A great and wise philosopher once said that not all hands extended are extended to help and save. Some are extended to grasp, destroy, and devour.

I am not here to tell you only you want to hear. I am here to tell you the truth. Whether you listen or not that is your choice. The truth is in this time of our dire spiritual crisis there is a message each of us needs to hear. The message is simple, 'We must fight the good fight, we must finish the race, and we must remain faithful.'

The turmoil presented by the continually humiliating saga of Christian greed and corruption has revealed a number of fake and false prophets in the midst of the children of God. These prophets and teachers confused us with their worldly wisdom and delighted us with their satanic intentions simply because we did not read the word of God for ourselves.

Regardless of the intentions of the individuals involved, one fact constantly rings true. That fact is all things work together for the good of those who love God according to God's purpose. God brought these things to path so each of us will better understand that our soul salvation is important. It is important to God and it is important to Lucifer. Because of this importance, we need to be on our constant guard against the enemy that tries to guide us down the wrong path.

Sometimes, God must guide us to a place of standing still

and coast us to lie down in our faith that He alone is capable and able to provide just what we need to do his work. Because of the spiritual importance of our soul salvation, we must become determined to work out our own soul's salvation with fear and with trembling. We do not get to do life over and God does not accept excuses because life is an open book test. So open the book, and read His instructions. Then work out your own salvation knowing that if you miss heaven the only person to blame will be you.

Therefore, when we judge our spiritual leaders and others to be lying, to be crooks, and to be dishonest, we in turn are simply judging ourselves. When we determine the teachings of our spiritual leaders to be false, we unwisely do not realize the statements that we are making are not only about our spiritual leaders. They are statements about us, spiritually as well. Since everything we believe was taught to us by a so-called false prophet, then that makes everything we believe false. In addition, that makes each of us followers of a false prophet.

Now instead of getting mad and allowing Lucifer to continue to drag us down into sin, repent for the kingdom of God is at hand. Repent for not reading the Word of God for ourselves. Repent for chasing after the wisdom of man and not asking for the wisdom from God. We need to re-evaluate our spiritual mistake of not verifying what we are led to believe is what the Word of God tell us to believe. We will answer one day for what we do and whom we believe.

Please let us collectively lift our eyes to the hills from whence comes our help. Our help will come only from God, because God has already made plans to deliver each person from this Christian nightmare. Open the Scriptures and then let the Holy Spirit of God lead, guide and teach us everything we will need to know. The wisdom of man is foolishness unto God. God said, “Do not make the image or likeness of anything in heaven on earth or under the earth. Do not worship or bow down to it.” Yet, we raised our idol in form of praying hands in agreement to everything these false prophets told us. We gladly swallow their con game of selling God’s blessings for a dollar bill completely.

So in reality, this loudly demonstrates that we do not understand the words the Scriptures are saying. We do not know what you should believe. God’s Word definitely did not state that we could buy or sell the blessing of God. It does not tell us that if we could give a preacher, church organization or anyone $100 then God would give it back to us ten folds, one hundred folds, or even one thousand folds. However, the Scriptures do state that giving to the poor is like lending to the Lord. Nevertheless, before you believe even those words I say check it out in the Scripture for yourself.

The point that I am trying to make is we hurry to listen to what man; sinful man says we should be like as the children of God and forget to check with God who called us his children first. Then we are turned over to a reprobate mind. We start hating the ways of God. We start chasing after Mammon, itself. We forgot we could not serve two masters, God and Mammon (money). We will either love one or hate the other. If we choose to love Mammon instead of God, the Word of God states that the love of money (Mammon) is the root of all evil.

I bet all of us who took to the prosperity false teaching wish that we had read and understood Matthew 19: 16-30 for ourselves. All we had to do was open the book called the SCRIPTURES and ask God to reveal what Jesus said. We need to wake up because our salvation is on line. Do we believe in God or the one whom we hired to be the preacher? Paul said in Acts chapter 17 and verse 24-25 that God does not dwell in the houses made by man. Instead, he dwells in the hearts of his people. The Scriptures correctly predicted this day would come. It is here. It is the day when even the elect of God will be fooled, except God shortens the last days.

Nevertheless, we continue to build brick and stone building to block in God. We continually listen to the false Prophets. We are continually deceived by their well-spoken words and degrees. However, the Scripture clearly states that man's wisdom is foolishness to God. Yet, how many of our churches or us will elect a pastor that does not have a long line of abbreviations behind their names. How many of us now feel stupid for believing the things these false prophets told us.

We have been erroneously led to believe that if we give $100 then God will bless us. However, we fail to realize that every day we are graced to wake up on this side of the grave, we are blessed. Furthermore, we continue to bring our hard-earned money to their coffers. The question now is will we continue to let the false prophets fool us into robbing God of his tithes and offering. On the other hand, will we go find someone, not some organization rather someone in need and help him or her with our tithes? Will we help them so there might be meat in their house? (Made in God image and likeness with the spirit of God dwelling inside) Then and only then will God open the windows of heaven and pour us out a blessing that we will not have room enough to receive. Therefore, if we want to really tithe to God, we should first give to the poor, needy, and the less fortunate.

'When I was in jail you visited me not' is the words our savior will repeat to many of us. Our answer will be, 'But God we gave to the Salvation Army and YMCA, and all the organizations we decided to set up to do this.' 'Did I say that these organizations did not? I said YOU did not.' our savior will reply. 'But Lord, we healed and cast out demon in your name through our church building pastors and chosen leaders', we will helplessly reason. Sadly, God will reply, 'Get the away from me you workers of iniquity for I know you not.'

God only knows those that seek to know him. He does not know those that send someone else to find out and then gladly pay him or her to tell to them about him whom they should have sought out themselves. The scripture does not say send our pastors and chosen leaders to seek me and you will find me. It loudly states if you seek me; then you shall find me. Let us resolve in ourselves to do our own seeking. Let us resolve in ourselves to come to our own understanding because if we are fooled it is our own fault.

One more thing I would like to express to us, The Scriptures instruct us to worship God in spirit and in truth. If I tell you to stand and pray or tell you to worship when I say to worship, how is this worshiping God in spirit and in truth. The Scriptures states 'Give not grudgingly nor of necessity for God love a cheerful giver.' However, if I teach you to give because the church building needs this or that, then that giving is of necessity. If I tell you to give or God will not bless you, then that giving is grudgingly. Do not be fooled and miss your blessings for the giving that God has blessed you to do. Give only because you love God so much you just want to show him how cheerful you are that He blessed you to be on this side of the grave for one more day.

Let us put down the books written by man. Let us dismiss the wisdom the world tries to give us. Let us look only to the hills from which comes our help. Our help, knowledge, and wisdom come only from God, not through colleges, Seminaries (religious schools) or church conferences. Our help only comes from God.

However, just as God is faithful to allow the sun to rise over the distant horizon everyday on time, He is capable of bringing us through these nights of chastisements that we must endure. We must endure them because we know the truth; however, we chose to follow a lie. We must endure them because every false prophet God warned us about we fell for. Nevertheless, God will bring us through.

Just as surely as God created a sun uncountable years ago to warm and light the earth on every new day, He has provide a way out for us. The darkness of the chastising recession is charging violently and forcefully over the horizon to devour the economy of our planet. Nevertheless, let us remember that God did not give us the spirit of fear but the spirit of power, love, and a sound mind. Always bear in mind that God will not put more on us than we can bare and He will always provide a way of escape.

Growing in Christ for the successful life

Romans 5: 1-11; 1 Corinthians 3: 1-4; Hebrews 6: 1-3

I wish I could say that we, the children of God, have matured in our faith walk with God and now stand ready for the great harvest. However, the evidence before us reveals that we are still mere infants in our faith walk. As new believers just reborn from a life of sin, we ventured into the comforts of the church building, God's schoolhouse. Inside the church building, we feasted on the milk of the gospel and learned of the rules and ways of God. As the children of God and through our selected pastors and teachers, the Holy Spirit taught us and some of us did learn that just like in carnal life, the children of God must work as well as learn the lessons. We must work out our soul's salvation with fear and trembling, so we can grow up to affect the world outside the schoolhouse.

As we feasted upon the word of God, we matured in our faith inside the walls of the schoolhouse. We nourished on the gospel as we grew up in our faith. We learned about the forbidden sins of life, like jealously, hatred and lust. We understood the wages of these and other sins equated to our death. Inside the treasured halls of our denominational schoolhouses, we learned the tenets of our faith in God. We received divine revelations about the purpose of God that ushered us into a spiritual relationship with God.

However, it is hurtfully evident that carnal and corrupt forces continue to control the household of God. As babes in Christ, we received the beneficial principles of faith from the table of God. Yet, as the maturing children of God, some of us neglected to dine upon the meat of wisdom and understanding that comes with the word of God. Now as carnal-minded men and women, we are proud of our worldly wisdom, knowledge, and self-conceit. Still, our minute desire for the meat of the knowledge and wisdom of

God has left us underdeveloped, spotted, and blemished. The Holy Spirit cannot communicate the deep things of God to us because we exist as malnourished men and women of God. Our spiritual stomachs cannot digest the meat of the gospel because we prefer the milk of the gospel.

Nevertheless, it is the God-appointed duty of every faithful pastor, teacher, and other ministers of the gospel of Christ to make sure that every hearer of the word of God under their care grow up and bear fruit. In the carnal world, we strive to make sure our babies develop into educated men and women. We educate them in hopes of them growing up to be productive citizens. In the spiritual household of God, God expects every child to grow. God expects us to develop and become productive men and women of God.

Ministers of God, God will hold us accountable if we do not endeavor to make sure those under our care grow in godly wisdom and knowledge. God placed the gifts of ministry and offices of leadership in the organized church for the perfecting or maturing of the saints. In the schoolhouse of God, we mature by eating the meat of the gospel. The meat of the gospel enables the child of God to develop into the men and women of God. As men and women of God, we are no longer children in understanding. We are neither weak in our faith, nor inconstant in our judgments because we are perfecting or maturing.

As the maturing children of God, we must grow up in all things. We must become deeply rooted in God. God expects us to increase in love, knowledge, works, and faith. As we eat the maturing meat of the gospel and perform the work of God, we increase in our love, faith, and dependence upon God. The more we increase or become perfected in every grace, the more we honor our head. But how do we grow? We mature in our faith walk when we assist, help, and view one to another as members of the household of God. We mature when we understand that we receive the Fruit of the Spirit from Christ for the sake and benefit of the entire body of Christ.

There are nine characteristic of the mature man or woman of God. These fruits of the Holy Spirit are love, joy, peace, longsuffering, gentleness, goodness, faith, meekness and temperance. These are not individual gifts. They are the physical manifestation of a righteous lifestyle. In order to mature from the children of God into the men and women of God, we should endeavor to develop these characteristics.

When it comes to our faith walk, we as fallible humans must remember something. We are to help everyone in need. It is not up to us to decide who deserved it, or who do not. We are commissioned or gifted in help. During our missions of help, we must not focus on ourselves. Our perspective must be concurrent with that of Christ. 'My command is this: Love each other as I have loved you. Greater love has no one than this that he lays down his life for his friends. You are my friends if you do what I command. I no longer call you servants, because a servant does not know his master's business. Instead, I have called you friends, for everything that I learned from my Father, I have made known to you. You did not choose me, but I chose you and appointed you to go and bear fruit—fruit that will last. Then the Father will give you whatever you ask in my name. This is my command: Love each other.'

Only when we help others, do we receive the help that we really need. Foremost, as fallible humans, we were in a state of helplessness because we are born in sin. However, because we were helpless to save ourselves, Christ died for us. Still, as David stated in Psalm 37: 25-26, 'I was young and now I am old, yet I have never seen the righteous forsaken or their children begging bread. They are always generous and lend freely; their children will be blessed.' In addition, Jesus gives us the promise that should calm our nerves. He promised, 'Then the Father will give you whatever you ask in my name. This is my command: Love each other.' We receive this blessing when we give freely of ourselves to help others. Whether the help we render is monetary, physical, or spiritual, remember, those that give to the poor lend to the Lord.

Now since we are his friends, Jesus expects us to do the same. However, because of our carnal nature, we tend to put limitations on this Christ-like love or giving. We tend to be of the opinion that God has commissioned us to do certain things that we do not have to do, or we cannot do everything expected of us by God. This could not be further from the truth. We are sent to help those in need of help. We are sent to lay down our lives so others may rise up. We are sent to be the very image and likeness of God in this world.

In John 14: 12-14 Jesus said, 'I tell you the truth, anyone who has faith in me will do what I have been doing. He will do even greater things than these, because I am going to the Father. And I will do whatever you ask in my name, so that the Son may bring glory to the Father. You may ask me for anything in my name, and I will do it.' So, this means that we no longer have to be afraid of giving or doing as God has instructed us. Because we are Christ-like, we are to do the same things. We are to do even greater things than the things that Christ did. Moreover, when we need help along the way, we are assured that we can ask of God, and he will give it to us according to his riches in glory.

Looking America in the face

Because I was born on July 9, 1964 on Lakeland Farms in rural Perry County, the early years of my life were filled with the evidence of the racial prejudices and the demeaning injustices that we faced as African Americans. For the first sixteen of my life, I was forced to recognize the fact that I truly lived in a segregated society. I grew up in a mostly African American community where my grandfather worked on a dairy farm. Often I would witness him refer to various Caucasians as mister or madam, even though he would be much older than they would be. I attended a segregated school and worshipped at a segregated church where the usual topics of discussion included some references of how the American society was treating us as a people. In spite of the words that I learned to repeat as I faced the American flag, in reality, I came to understand that I lived in a country that was actually many different nations under God. I came to realize this country was divided. Moreover, I came to realize that it offered liberty and justice only to those that belonged to the desired race and/or had enough money to purchase it.

As I left the comforts and seclusion of my small rural beginnings in 1981 to venture into the vast world, my heart was filled with the hope of discovering the America that I was taught about in school. I yearned to find the America that was shaped by the idea that all men were created equal. I yearned to find the America that was built upon the foundation of liberty and justice for all. I left Alabama, moved to Miami with my mother, and enrolled in American Senior High School. Even though I would no longer face the unmistakable racism of rural Perry County, I soon discovered that in America, the preferred way of life was indeed segregation. Moreover, the America that I was taught about in school did not exist.

During the decades since I left rural Perry County, I have had the chance to travel this great country. The one thing that I see no matter where I go is we are still a country that has not fully erased the lines that divide us. When I wake up in the morning, I find myself waking up in an America that still encourages us to place separating barriers on ourselves. I wake up to an America that is actually many nations, under many gods. I wake up to an America that has divided itself into many segregated communities of African Americans, Hispanic Americans, Japanese Americans, Irish Americans, Native Americans, and White Americans. I wake up to an America that offers liberty and justice to all only if they are of the desired race and/or have enough money to purchase it.

In the four and a half decades since the start of the American Civil Rights Movement and my birth, the American society has yet to come to grips with the words that the founding fathers of this country penned in the sacred pages of our constitution. These words mention something about us holding certain truths to be self-evident that all men are created equal and are endowed by God with certain right, which includes life, liberty and the pursuit of happiness. Even though these very words have been repeated and included in various sermons, commentaries, and articles, America remains at a complete loss to the real meaning of these words. Over the years, America has been constantly trying to reshape itself into the nation that is presented in the preamble. Yet for some reason, we have still fallen short. True, we have gotten rid of slavery and other injustices that were placed upon various minorities. Yet, we have picked up other injustices and now fight to make them a part of our permanent society.

Therefore, I must question how we can hold these truths to be self evident that all men are created equal. That all men are endowed by our creator to certain inalienable right that includes life, liberty and the pursuit of happiness, when these truths have not even become evident in our communities, business, organizations, or in our way of thinking. The only truths, in our society, that have become evident are that we are many different nations, that have divided ourselves into our own preferred segregated communities, and that we serve ethnically colored gods.

It has become plainly apparent that the motives of our modern day leaders have turned away from making sure that everyone regardless of race, creed, color, national origin, or economic status will be treated fairly in America. Their goal has now become one of making sure that only the rich and powerful is taken care of without regard to the condition of the rest of our fellow Americans. Their intention is to reintroducing into society the very same ideals of segregation that many fought so hard to get rid of in the first place. Their objective is for America to evolve into a society where jobs will be issued out according to wealth, power and influence rather than qualification. However, it is time for the American society to wake up and see that any kind of forced segregation need and should be a thing of the pass.

Today, the American society, in practice, has become even worse than the Jim Crow society of old was in reality. Today, we, the American society, continue to segregate ourselves from each other. Today, the rich and elite of the American society practice and possess the same misguided attitudes that African Americans had to endure from the white race for so long. Today, we, the American society, have taken up where the Klan left off years ago. We are killing ourselves and destroying our own neighborhoods. However, since the economic tide has turned, it is now time for us to put aside our outdated way of thinking and press forward to making the dream of Dr. King come true.

I assure you that the American society have not forgotten the many heroes of the past civil right struggle; nor have we forgotten the great price that was paid in blood, sweat, and tears for the freedom that America can claim today. Instead, we, the American society, must now wake from our dreams of a bright future that was teeming with opportunities to excel. We must now face the reality of an American society that has become broke because of the overwhelming greed of the rich and elite and our desire to segregate ourselves. In order for the American society to become a great country, then we, America as a whole, must come to understand just what the words we hold so dear really do mean. They mean that if America is one nation under God then it must also be in God. We must possess the same opinion of the God that we say we serve. We must be colorblind just as God is colorblind. We must possess the ability to see each other not as African Americans, Hispanic Americans, White Americans, or even rich, middle class, or poor Americans rather just as Americans.

Nevertheless, my fellows American, as we press forward into the unsure future, let us not forget to look at the past. When we look, let us not look through the glasses that have been shaped by racism or grounded in hatred for our brothers and sisters. Rather let us peer through the same spectacles of hope that our ancestors wore when they first envisioned this country. Rather let us peer through the same spectacles of faith that Dr. King and many others of all races use during the Civil Rights Movement. Let us peer through the same spectacles of hope and faith into the self-evident truth that as long as we realize that we are all a part of the body of Christ there will never exist a wall big, wide, or strong enough to hold America back from become the great country that God has called for it to be. A country where we realize that we are all created equal by one God and given the inalienable rights to life, liberty, and the pursuit of happiness. Then as Dr. King said, "Then we can all join hands and sing with new meaning the words of the old Negro Spiritual ‘Free at last, free at last, thank God, Almighty, America is free at last.

www.ingramcontent.com/pod-product-compliance
Ingram Content Group UK Ltd.
Pitfield, Milton Keynes, MK11 3LW, UK
UKHW041919190726
13854UKWH00003B/1327

9 781458 372864